Declare The Word Of God

Faith Confessions
For Daily Living

Declare The Word Of God

Faith Confessions For Daily Living

Carla Strogen

All scripture quotations are taken from the King James Version of the Bible.
Declare The Word of God
Faith Confessions For Daily Living

ISBN:
Copyright: 2021 Carla Strogen
Layout: Ines Rychlewska

Printed in the United States of America.

All rights reserved. This material is protected by the United States copyright laws. No part of this publication may be reproduced, stored in a retrieval system or transmitted in any form or by any means, electronic, mechanical or photocopying, recording, or otherwise without the prior permission of the publisher.

Contents

Introduction	7
Destiny	9
Don't Quit	13
Faith	18
Favor	23
God Is With You	28
Manifestations	33
Obstacles	38
Situations	45
Victory	51
Waiting on God	56
Wisdom	60
Words	64
Conclusion	70
Praise Scriptures	71
Fruit of The Spirit	74
Divine Name of God	84

Introduction

For the law of the Spirit of life in Christ Jesus hath made me free from the law of sin and death.

[Romans 8:2]

Confessing the word of God is what I do daily. There are many challenges and issues that we have to deal with in life, but how you deal with them will determine your end result. You may try to take other avenues, but those things will never work when it comes to applying them to your situations and circumstances. Try the word of God, it is the only thing that will give the desired results.

Confessing the word of God is very important. The word of God will get you through anything. You are waiting for God to do everything, when it is your responsibility. You have to do something. God is waiting on you to do your part.

"If it is going to be, it is up to you"

Destiny

Your destiny is not determined by your setbacks or your current situations, but have faith in God. Expect your situations to change. You must trust God, and lean not unto your own understanding, but as you acknowledge him in all your ways and let him direct your paths. What you think is best, may not be what you need.

Confession

Declare, for God know the thoughts that he think toward me; thoughts of peace, and not of evil, to give me an expected end, then shall I call upon him, and I shall go and pray unto him, and he will hearken unto me.

[Jeremiah 29:11,12]

DESTINY

It may take longer to reach your destination, but that does not mean you will not get there. You just have to take a different route, but you will reach it if you don't quit before time. Continue to have persistence, determination and perseverance. Your pathway may be different than others, but stay connected to the Everlasting Father, the Mighty God, the only Living and True God; he will always come through for you.

Confession

Declare, I will not be weary in well doing: for in due season I shall reap, because I will not faint.

[Galatians 6:9]

God knows how to get you where you need to be. Why? Because he is Omniscient (all-knowing). When one door closes, pray that the right door opens. Just know he has something better for you. You might not understand everything at the time, but you have to trust God that he will give you favor with man, and he will put the right person in your path to help you.

Confession

Declare, Great is our Lord, and of great power: his understanding is infinite.

[Psalm 147:5]

Tell yourself everything will be alright. The best is yet to come. Expect it. The place you are in now; you must believe it is not where you are going to stay. Continue to confess where you want to go, and what you want to receive; eventually you will see the manifestation of your confession. Expect promotions and increase, you can have it.

Confession

Declare, now unto him that is able to do exceeding abundantly above all that I ask or think, according to the power that worketh in me.

[Ephesians 3:20]

Don't Quit

When it looks like nothing is happening for you, and nothing you are believing for is manifesting. Don't fret. Don't let time discourage you from anticipating the promise. God has not forgotten about you. He knows just what to do, and when to do it.

Confession

Declare, I will not fear, because God is with me. I am not dismayed; for God will strengthen me; yea he will help me; yea, he will uphold me with the right hand of his righteous.

[Isaiah 41:10]

No matter how hard it is, or no matter how hard it gets; you can't give up. Don't quit. You can overcome this test. You will not be defeated. Remember, you always win. You might be overwhelmed right now, and the problem is very hard to bear, but God said for the joy of the Lord is your strength. He has already given you the victory.

Confession

Declare, I am strong in the Lord, and in the power of his might.

[Ephesians 6:10]

You might be in an uncomfortable place now, but don't give up before the blessing manifest. Thank God you have moved from this too shall pass, to and it came to pass.

Confession

Declare, I will be of good courage, and he shall strengthen my heart, because I hope in the Lord.

[Psalm 31:24]

Don't focus on the past, move on. Expect greater and better days. God is a restorer. You might have made mistakes in areas of your life, that has cause some setbacks, but that does not stop the blessings God has for you. You didn't get the response you were expecting the first time, but keep trying until you get what you want. Don't let a negative response deter you; be determined that you will not stop until you get the right response.

Confession

Declare, I will seek first the kingdom of God and his righteousness, and all these things will be added to me.

[Matthew 6:33]

Are you saying, Lord will this ever end? Be encouraged, I say yes it will. You have been waiting a long time for your breakthrough, but don't quit. Time can cause you to become discourage because you are doing all the right things, and still seem like you can't get a break. Continue to keep doing what is right, and your time will come. You will be glad you waited.

Confession

Declare, I will not cast away my confidence, which hath great recompense of reward.

[Hebrews 10:35]

Faith

Faith is not an option. Faith is a requirement, release your faith to access the promise. We live by faith, not by sight. Faith is the only way you will obtain the promises of God. Faith is what pleases God. Faith comes by hearing, and hearing the word of God. So that means you have to keep hearing and hearing and hearing the word over in order for faith to come. So continue to decree and declare by faith, it's already done. It's already yours. Say it's already done. It's already yours.

Confession

Declare, I have now faith, because now faith is the substance of things hoped for, the evidence of things not seen.

[Hebrews 11:1]

If God said it, you must believe in order to receive it. No matter what it looks like, or feel like. You will get discouraged. You will shed some tears, but you still have to stand firm in your faith. You have to be alert, be courageous, and be strong. You have to endure to the end. Declare I am a faith walker, I walk by faith and I talk faith.

Confession

Declare, but without faith it is impossible to please him: for he that cometh to God must believe that he is, and that he is a rewarder of them that diligently seek him.

[Hebrews 11:6]

FAITH

Continue to have faith in God in difficult times. God will give you the strength to endure, and faith to maintain until you receive what you are believing for. By faith, you will obtain the promise. If you can believe what your husband, children, brother, sister, auntie, uncle, cousin, boss, or even someone you do know tell you. What about God? Have faith in God, he never lies.

Confession

Declare, God is my refuge and strength, a very present help in trouble.

[Psalm 46:1]

You must believe good things will happen for you. Believe you are coming out of your situation. You do not have to accept nothing less than the best. Your struggle is not who you are. This too shall pass, and you don't have to settle, by faith expect God's best. He wants you to prosper in every area of your life; whether it is spiritually, financially, relational or emotionally. Every area means every area, nothing missing, nothing broken.

Confession

Declare, beloved, God wish above all things that I mayest prosper and be in health, even as my soul prospereth.

[3 John 2]

FAITH

Be encourage, I don't know your story, but one thing I do know is that God is faithful to his word. Your faith has brought you through many situations and circumstances, and it will bring you through this. You can say, if it has not been for the Lord on my side where would I be. So, you know what God has brought you through, and where God has brought you from. Be encouraged.

Confession

Declare, it is the Lord's mercies that I am not consumed, because his compassions fail not.

[Lamentations 3:22]

Favor

God's favor will open doors for you that no man can shut. God's favor exceeds your talents, your education and your experience. Favor goes beyond your credentials. Some positions you would not have gotten, if God did not move on your behalf. God can place you in positions that you don't even qualify for, but the favor of God qualified you.

Confession

Declare, I walk in the favor of God because, he will openeth doors for me that no man shutteth, and he shutteth doors, and no man openeth.

[Revelation 3:7]

FAVOR

The blessing God has for you will not pass you by. What God has for you it is for you, and nothing and no one can stop it when it is your set time of favor. Man's no can't stop God yes. It not what he says, she says or they say. God has the final say. No matter how many denials you get, it will happen. God will place the right people in your path at the right time just to bless you.

Confession

Declare, my eyes have not seen, nor my ears heard, neither have entered into my heart the things which God hath prepared for me because I love him.

[1 Corinthians 2:9]

They said you couldn't have it, but God says IT'S YOURS. They said you wouldn't make it, but God says YES YOU WILL. They said you couldn't do it, but God says YES YOU CAN. Don't let people tell you what you can and can't have; if it is based on the word of God, you can have it. If you meet the conditions according the word of God, you can have it.

Confession

Declare, so shall God's word that goeth forth out of my mouth: it shall not return unto me void, but it shall accomplish that which I please, and it shall prosper in the thing whereto I sent it.

[Isaiah 55:11]

Remember, what God has for you, no one can delay it, deny it or stop it. You have to remain faithful to the word of God. Sometimes people are jealous of you, and they will do any and everything to try to hinder your blessing, but with God on your side it will not work. God is Omnipotent (all powerful), man is no match when it comes to God.

Confession

Declare, I have overcome them: because greater is he that is in me, than he that is in the world.

[1 John 4:4]

You must expect God to arrange things in your favor. Even if everything is total opposite from what you are believing for. You might be experiencing problem after problem. Seem like when you get a step ahead, and you get pushed back. Stay focus on the promise; in spite of what you see.

Confession

Declare, the Lord shall command the blessing upon me, in my storehouses, and in all that I settest my hand to; and he shall bless me in the land.

[Deuteronomy 28:8]

God Is With You

What you can't do, God can. He takes what looks impossible and makes possible. You don't have to try to figure it out, just trust God, and know that he has already worked it out. What you see in the natural can be very disappointing, but stand strong. God is right there with you every step of the way.

Confession

Declare, with men this is impossible; but with God all things are possible.

[Matthew 19:26]

The enemy will try to get you to believe nothing is working for you, but God will never leave you, nor forsake you. He is with you through the hard times. Sometimes you don't know how strong you are; until strong is all you have to be in order to make it. You are stronger than you think. God will not put too much on you than you can bare.

Confession

Declare, God will never leave me, nor forsake me.

[Hebrews 13:5]

You can't do it in your own strength. You might say how much more of this can I handle. Nothing seems to be going right for you. Confusion is all around. You say, I am tired of going through the same situations over and over, but with God's help, he will sustain you. He will keep you, and he will protect you.

Confession

Declare, I will cast my burden upon the Lord,
and he shall sustain me: he shall never suffer the righteous to be moved.

[Psalm 55:22]

Let God be, I AM that I AM for you. Whatever you need him to be he will be just that. He is your DELIVER, GUIDANCE, GRACE, GREATER, HEALER, LOVE, MENDER OF A BROKEN HEART, MORE THAN ENOUGH, PEACE, PROVIDER, PROTECTOR, REFUGE, WAYMAKER, WISDOM, STRENGTH, SAFETY, AND SO MUCH MORE.

Confession

Declare, God is I AM THAT I AM in my life.

[Exodus 3:14]

You can rely on God. He is able to meet every one of your needs. He is your Jehovah Jireh. If you are a giver, he said give, and it shall be given unto you; good measure, pressed down, and shaken together, and running over, shall men give into your bosom. For the same measure that ye mete withal it shall be measured to you again. Be a sower, and not just a receiver. So when you give, expect a return on your seed.

Confession

Declare, but my God shall supply all my need according to his riches in glory by Christ Jesus.

[Philippians 4:19]

Manifestations

When God says yes, everything else is irrelevant. He supersedes everything and everyone. Nothing or no one can prevent your blessing from manifesting, but you can. If you do not follow the biblical principles that is set in place. If you do your part, God will do the rest.

Confession

Declare, for all the promises of God in him are yea, and in him Amen, unto the glory of God by us.

[2 Corinthians 1:20]

You must let God lead and guide you in all affairs of your life. Let his plans and purposed be established. Don't rely on your own understanding, trust God. His plans are the only plans that will succeed. Ask God for directions, he will give you the answers you need, if you listen. He will tell you what to do, and what not to do, if you listen. Holy Spirit will lead and guide you into all truth, if you listen. LISTENING IS THE KEY.

Confession

Declare, for God know the thoughts that he think toward me, saith the Lord, thoughts of peace, and not of evil, to give me an expected end.

[Jeremiah 29:11]

You know if God did it before. You can trust him to answer your prayers again. This is nothing that God can't handle. He said, be careful (anxious) for nothing; but in everything by prayer and supplication with thanksgiving let your requests be made known unto him. So, once you have prayed about it, began to praise and thank him for the manifestation. Praise him, praise him, praise him, and thank him, thank him, thank him.

Confession

Declare, I will ask, and it shall be given unto me; I will seek, and I shall find; I will knock, and it shall be opened unto me.

[Matthew 7:7]

You might not know how, when or where God will answer, but just know he will answer. As long as you keep believing, and keep confessing the word; you will have a BUT GOD testimony. He will do it for you. It will be well worth the wait. It will be well worth the wait. He will give you more than you thought you would ever receive. Declare, I have a BUT GOD testimony.

Confession

Declare, I will delight myself in the Lord; and he shall give me the desires of my heart.

[Psalm 37:4]

Expect favor, breakthroughs and manifestations of your prayers. Confess you are moving to better, and greater things in your life. You have to get a picture in your mind, and see yourself with the desired promises. Write your vision down, and keep it before you. Put it up where you can see it, and declare that you have what you say.

Confession

Declare, and the Lord shall make me the head, and not the tail; and I shall be above only, and I shalt not be beneath; if I hearken unto the commandments of the Lord my God, which he commands me this day, to observe and to do them.

[Deuteronomy 28:13]

Obstacles

You can overcome any obstacle that you are faced with. Why? Because God says you can. No matter what it looks like in the natural. No matter what situation you go through, know God is able to deliver. It might seem like you will never come out of a particular situation, but you will if you are determined not to remain in that situation. I am a witness, no matter how big your problem seems, if you keep your eyes on God he will deliver you out every time.

Confession

Declare, the Lord is my strength and my shield; my heart trusted in me, and I am helped: therefore, my heart greatly rejoiceth; and with my song will I praise him.

[Psalm 28:7]

Don't let what you are going through now, dictate what you will receive. You must know that is not the end result. It's yours, just believe you can have it. Just look back on all the times, you prayed and your prayers was answered.

Confession

Declare, I calleth those things which be not as though they were.

[Romans 4:17]

OBSTACLES

If God brought you out before, he can and will do it again. He is faithful. You stay focus, and don't get distracted. Keep your eyes on moving forward, to the place you want to be. Press your way through it all, and you will be glad you did.

Confession

Declare, Jesus Christ the same yesterday, today and forever.

[Hebrews 13:8]

Give your problems to God. Let him do it. Push through, the pain and the tears. You will make it. It is hard right now, but your good days will always outweigh your bad days. Even if it does not seem like it right now. You still have a lot to be thankful for.

Confession

Declare, I am born of God therefore I overcometh the world: and this is the victory that overcometh the world, even my faith.

[1 John 5:4]

OBSTACLES

You must keep persevering in times of adversity. Continue to stay strong in your faith, and endure until the end. God is greater. You can do it. It might be overwhelming now, but it will all work together in the end.

Confession

Declare, I will beareth all things, believeth all things, hopeth all things, endureth all things.

[1 Corinthians 13:7]

Don't look back at what you could have or should have done. Those things you done in the past can't be changed. Keep moving forward, believe your best days are ahead of you. Focus on what you can do now to change your life. If you keep looking back at the past, your future will always be hindered. The only time to look back is to thank God for what he brought you out of. Don't let your past be a stumbling block for your future.

Confession

Declare, I will not remember the former things, neither consider the things of old because God does not.

[Isaiah 43:18]

OBSTACLES

When it seems like nothing is changing and problems continue. You are at your lowest point, and you don't think it is worth it anymore. You must remain consistent in the word of God, and by faith continue to speak victory over your situation and circumstances. Confess you are a warrior and a champion, and you will not give up easily.

Confession

Declare, no in all these things I am more than a conqueror through him who loved me.

[Romans 8:37]

Situations

What does the word of God say about your situation? Speak what you desire because you have what you say. You can hinder your own blessing by what you are saying. Are you speaking words of faith or words of doubt? Your words have power. When you speak words out your mouth in the atmosphere, you are setting in motion what you will receive. You must make sure you speak words of faith.

Confession

Declare, I will not speak death to my situation, but I will speak life to my situation because death and life are in the power of my tongue: and I shalt eat the fruit thereof whether it is good or bad.

[Proverbs 18:21]

SITUATIONS

No matter what the situation appears to be in the natural realm, you must see pass what is happening, and claim I am victorious. It may be totally opposite to what you are wanting to see manifest, but you still have to speak what the word says about it. You have come too far to give up now. Don't quit until you see change.

Confession

Declare, but thanks be to God, which giveth me the victory through our Lord Jesus Christ.

[1 Corinthians 15:57]

Your current situation does not dictate your final destination. Through your disappointment, challenges and setback, keep moving forward. You must keep walking by faith until you reach your set goal. By faith, your latter will be greater than your former.

Confession

Declare, behold the Lord will do a new thing; now it shall spring forth; shall ye not know it? God will make a way in the wilderness, and rivers in the desert.

[Isaiah 43:19]

SITUATIONS

Don't be controlled by your situations and circumstances, but you must control them by what you say and do. Say it is already better, and move in the direction you need to go in in order for change to happen. Keep saying it, until you see it. You can't just sit around and do nothing, and just expect something to happen. It does not work like that. You do your part, and then something happens. God will step in and do what you can't.

Confession

Declare, I shall say unto this mountain, be thou removed, and cast into the sea; and I shall not doubt in my heart, but shall believe that those things which I saith shall come to pass; I shall have whatsoever I saith.

[Mark 11:23]

You have made it through some tough times, and this too shall pass. You didn't know how you was going to get through some of those times either, but you have survived some of the roughest experiences in your life. You are a fighter. Believe it is so, and it shall be. Believe it is so, and it shall be. Believe it is so, and it shall be. You have to make confessions over and over and over and over again.

Confession

Declare, whatever I shall ask in prayer, I believe, I shall receive.

[Matthew 21:22]

SITUATIONS

During your difficult times just remember, what you have already overcame. Trust God no matter what. He will see you through the difficult times. When you feel like you are all alone, he is right there to comfort you. He will be your peace that surpasses all understanding. You don't understand why things happen the way they do, but God is still God. He never changes. You change, people change, but God never changes.

Confession

Declare, God is my refuge and strength, a very present help in trouble.

[Psalm 46:1]

Victory

You are destined to walk in victory, no matter what you are experiencing at this present moment. Don't you stop expecting, keep expecting. You know what God can do, he has shown himself to be faithful to you every time you have needed him to move on your behalf. Victory, victory is yours. Victory, victory is yours.

Confession

Declare, the Lord my God is he that goeth with me, to fight for me against my enemies, to save me.

[Deuteronomy 20:4]

VICTORY

God can, will and is able to win every battle you encounter. How you handle the problems determines your outcome. Put your armor on, and fight the good fight of faith. Change can only happen, when you expect change.

Confession

Declare, my soul wait thou only upon god; for my expectation is from him.

[Psalm 62:5]

You did not come this far by faith, and not obtain the victory. You must let God fight your battles, and not do it yourself. Don't rely on your own understanding, it is too big for you to handle. Remember God is greater than the giants you face. Ask David, he will tell you how God handled Goliath. Let God slay your Goliath. He knows how to get it done with no struggle and no strain.

Confession

Declare, now thanks be unto God, which always causeth me to triumph in Christ.

[2 Corinthians 2:14]

VICTORY

Reminder, in spite of the disappointments, frustrations, and setbacks. You are still destined for victory. Don't move away from what you are doing, you keep doing it God's way and everything will be alright. God word will always get you where you need to be. In this world you will always have tribulations, but the good thing about it, you don't have to stand alone. You have God, the Father. Jesus Christ, the Son. Holy Spirit, the Comforter, and Angels, ministering spirits to back you. You have all the help you need.

Confession

Declare, I have peace in God. In this world I shall have tribulation; but I will be of good cheer; I have overcome.

[John 16:33]

You might not be where you want to be right now, but thank God you are not where you use to be. He has brought you from a mighty long way. You have more now than you have ever had in your life. So, thank him for what you already have. He will bring you out of this too. You win.

Confession

Declare, I will lift my eyes unto the hills from whence comet my help. My help cometh from the Lord, which made heaven and earth.

[Psalm 121:1,2]

Waiting on God

In your season of waiting, God is working all things together for your good because he said it would because you love him. Keep believing. It's working. Continue to stand on the word of God, and don't back down. Remember God's timing is not your timing, but he is always on time.

Confession

Declare, the Lord will perfect that which concerneth me; his mercy, O Lord, endureth forever: forsake not the works of thine own hands.

[Psalm 138:8]

Don't let time discourage you from receiving the promises, you may have been waiting a long time. It may take days, months or even sometimes years before you see the manifestation. But, while you wait expect to see the desired result.

Confession

Declare, and this is the confidence that I have in him, that, if I ask anything according to his will, he heareth me. And if I know that he hear me, whatsoever I ask, I know that I have the petitions that I desired of him.

[1 John 5:14,15]

In order to possess what you want, you have to confess what you want. It does not matter how long it's been. Don't stop confessing the word of God. If you don't want it, then don't say it. Because you have what you say. Delays does not mean denial; it just means not yet.

Confession

Declare, the Lord is good to me because I wait for him, to my soul because I seek him.

[Lamentations 3:25]

God is working behind the scenes, and he is maneuvering things for you. The promises might be delayed, but not denied. Your times and your seasons are orchestrated by God. He knows what is best for you. When you wait on God, you will not have any regrets. You may be expecting a new job, new home, new vehicle, a husband, or wife, a promotion, a healing, a financial blessing, to lose weight, to have a baby, these are just to name a few. You can have all these things, but timing mean everything.

Confession

Declare, to everything there is a season, and a time to every purpose under the heaven, and I am willing to wait for my time.

[Ecclesiastes 3:1]

Wisdom

Get wisdom, adhere to wise teaching. One bad decision can change your whole life for the rest of your life. Don't be influenced by others, be able to stand even if you have to stand alone for what is right. Don't go with the majority just because they are doing it, but you choose to do the right thing because you know your choices is right.

Confession

Declare, I will not forsake wisdom, and wisdom shall preserve me: I love wisdom, and she shall keep me.

[Proverbs 4:6]

Integrity is doing the right thing even when no one is watching. Your actions and your values are important. Can you be trusted? Are you dependable? Are you honest? Ask yourself these questions, and see what your answers to these questions are. You have to be able to do what is right, even in unpopular situations. It's not always about the majority; sometimes you might be the minority in certain situations. Right is right, and wrong is wrong and you can't dress it up to fit your situation.

Confession

Declare, my integrity shall guide me because I am upright: but the perverseness of transgressors shall destroy them.

[Proverbs 11:3]

Don't let someone change who you are to become what they need. Don't settle just for a temporary decision. Choose good character. You can be popular, and still not have any character. Your reputation is bad because everyone knows your character. There is a saying, "If you stand for something, you'll be sure to fall for anything." Respect goes a long way.

Confession

Declare, I will not be deceived: evil communication (bad company) corrupt good manners.

[1 Corinthians 15:33]

You have to make sound and wise decisions. Your choices in life will determine what kind of results you will get in life. When you have the life and nature of God in you, your conscience will not permit you to do just anything. You should think before you act.

Confession

Declare, because I am in Christ, I am a new creature, old things are passed away; behold all things are become new.

[2 Corinthians 5:17]

Words

Your words are powerful, keep saying it until you see it. You must keep saying it by faith, my due season has manifested. Words are like seeds, you plant the word in your heart and water it daily. This is how you grow and go through trials victoriously.

Confession

Declare, I will not be weary in well doing: for in due season I shall reap, if I faint not.

[Galatians 6:9]

What you confess become your reality. In spite of, the problems and situations you encounter, you must choose to say what the word says. That's why it is important to find scriptures that relates to the situation you are dealing with. Only then, will you know how and what to confess the word concerning that situation.

Confession

Declare, I will delight myself in your statues; I will not forget your word.

[Psalm 119:16]

WORDS

Speak to the problem, and not about the problem. Speak life and speak positive words. Confess what you want to manifest, and not what you don't want. The more you talk about the problem, it will not change, but the more you tell God about your problem and confess the word then it changes. Let the word guide and enlightened you.

Confession

Declare, the word is a lamp to my feet and a light to my path.

[Psalm 119:105]

Don't talk defeat and failure, talk victory and overcomer. God has the ability and power to get you through anything. God is all powerful. It's whatever you say that will determine your outcome. You must refuse to talk defeat and failure, but talk victory and overcomer.

Confession

Declare, God's grace is sufficient for me: for his strength is made perfect in my weakness.

[2 Corinthians 12:9]

WORDS

You have to abide in the word (remain in the word of God). You have to act on the word of God (do what the word of God says). You have to agree with the word of God (accept what the word of God says). The word of God is the only thing that can change your situation. Everything else is only temporary. It will not last. The word of God stands forever. So confess the word only, nothing else.

Confession

Declare, I will abide in Jesus, and his words abide in me, I shall ask what I will, and it shall be done unto me.

[John 15:7]

In order for change to take place, you must speak faith filled words, no matter what you see, hear or feel. This is the only thing that will get results based on the word of God. So, when you speak faith filled words, expect.

Confession

Declare, I will ask in faith, I will not waver.

[James 1:6]

Conclusion

As you go through life, remember you can overcome any test, trial or temptation because you have the greater on the inside of you. Confessing the word of God is very important, this helps me when I am faced with adversity. It builds my faith and it gives me strength to go through tough times. The word of God is a necessity, so don't go a day without reading it. So, let confessing and reading the word of God become a part of your daily routine.

All scripture is given by inspiration of God, and is profitable for doctrine, for reproof, for correction, for instruction in righteousness.

[2 Timothy 3:16]

Praise Scriptures

When going through your trials and test, just began to confess these praise scriptures. Praise your way through, praise our way through.

Now unto the King eternal, immortal, invisible, the only wise God, be honour and glory for ever and ever. Amen.

[1 Timothy 1:17]

Thou are my God, and I will praise thee: thou are my God, I will exalt thee.

[Psalm 118:28]

PRAISE SCRIPTURES

O, Lord, thou are my God; I will exalt thee, I will praise thy name; for thou hast done wonderful things; thy counsels of old are faithfulness and truth.

[Isaiah 25:1]

I will praise thee, O Lord, with my whole heart; I will shew forth all thy marvelous works.

[Psalm 9:1]

The Lord is my strength and my shield; my heart trusted in him and I am helped: therefore my heart greatly rejoiceth; and with my song will I praise him.

[Psalm 28:7]

PRAISE SCRIPTURES

Because they lovingkindness is better than life, my lips shall praise thee. Thus will I bless thee while I live: I will lift up my hands in thy name.

[Psalm 63:3-4]

I will bless the Lord at all times: his praise shall continually be in my mouth.

[Psalm 34:1]

Praise ye the Lord, Blessed is the man that feareth the Lord, that delighteth greatly in his commandments. 2) His seed shall be mighty upon earth: the generation of the upright shall be blessed. 3) Wealth and riches shall be in his house: and his righteous endureth for ever. 4) Unto the upright there ariseth light in the darkness: he is gracious, and full of compassion, and righteous.

[Psalm 112:1-4]

Fruit of The Spirit

As saints you will have to let these fruit of the Spirit develop in our life while going through trials.

But the fruit of the Spirit is love, joy peace, longsuffering, gentleness, goodness, faith, 23) Meekness, temperance: against such there is no law.

[Galatians 5:22-23]

Love
an affection of the mind excited by beauty and worth of any kind, or by the qualities of an object which communicate pleasure, sensual or intellectual, benevolence, kindness, charity, affection.

For God so loved the world, that he gave his only begotten Son, that whosoever believeth in him should not perish, but have everlasting life.

[John 3:16]

Charity suffereth long, and is kind; charity envieth not: charity vaunteth not itself, is not puffed up, 5) Doth not behave itself unseemly, seeketh not her own, it not easily provoked, thinketh no evil.

[1 Corinthians 13:4-5]

Let all your things be done with charity.

[1 Corinthians 16:14]

FRUIT OF THE SPIRIT

Joy
the passion or emotion excited by the acquisition or expectation of good that excitement of pleasurable feelings which is caused by success, gratification of desire or some good possessed.

The joy of the Lord is your strength.

[Nehemiah 8:1]

This is the day which the Lord hath made; we will rejoice and be glad in it.

[Psalm 118:24]

Thou wilt shew me the path of life: in thy presence is fullness of joy; at thy right hand there are pleasures forevermore.

[Psalm 16:11]

Peace
A state of quiet or transquillity freedom from disturbance or agitation applicable to society, to individuals, or to the temper of the mind, harmony.

The Lord bless thee, and keep thee: The Lord make his face shine upon thee, and be gracious unto the. The Lord lift up his countenance upon thee, and give thee peace.

[Numbers 6:24-26]

Thou wilt keep him in perfect peace, whose mind is stayed on thee: because he trusted in thee.

[Isaiah 26:3]

And the peace of God, which passeth all understanding, shall keep your hearts and minds through Christ Jesus.

[Philppians 4:7]

Longsuffering
bearing injuries or provocation (the act of exciting anger) for a long time; patient not easily provoked.

---

9) For this cause we also, since the day we heard it, do not cease to pray for you, and to desire that ye might be filled with the knowledge of his will in all wisdom and spiritual understanding; 10) That ye might be worthy of the Lord unto all pleasing, being fruitful in every good work, and increasing in the knowledge of God; 11) Strengthened with all might, according to his glorious power, unto all patience, and longsuffering with joyfulness. 12) Giving thanks unto the Father, which hath made us meet to be partakers of the inheritance of the saints in light: 13) Who hath delivered us from the power of darkness, and hath translated us into the kingdom of his dear Son: 14) In whom we have redemption through his blood, even the forgiveness of sins.

[Colossians 1:9-14]

Gentleness
softness of manners, mildness of temper sweetness of disposition; tenderness; mild treatment.

With all humility and gentleness, with patience, showing tolerance for one another in love.

[Ephesians 4:2]

Let your gentle spirit be known to all men. The Lord is near.

[Philippians 4:5]

A gentle answer turns away wrath, but a harsh word stirs up anger.

[Proverbs 15:1]

Goodness
favor shown; acts of kindness, the state of being good, the physical qualities which constitute value.

Trust in the Lord, and do good; so shalt thou dwell in the land, and verily thou shalt be fed.

[Psalm 37:3]

I had fainted, unless I had believed to see the goodness of the Lord in the land of the living.

[Psalm 27:13]

Depart from evil; and do good; seek peace, and pursue it.

[Psalm 34:14]

Faith
to trust, to persuade, to draw towards anything, to believe, to obey; confidence.

But without faith it is impossible to please him: for he that cometh to God must believe that he is, and that he is a rewarder of them that diligently seek him.

[Hebrews 11:6]

For we walk by faith, not by sight.

[2 Corinthians 5:7]

So then faith cometh by hearing, and hearing by the word of God.

[Romans 10:17]

Meekness
softness of temper, mildness, gentleness, forbearance.

But the meek shall inherit the earth; and shall delight themselves in the abundance of peace.

[Psalm 37:11]

For the Lord taketh pleasure in his people: he will beautify the meek with salvation.

[Psalm 149:4]

The meek will he guide in judgement: and the meek will he teach his way.

[Psalm 25:9]

Temperance
moderation in regard to the indulgence of the natural appetites and passions, restrained, self control.

Teaching us that, denying ungodliness and worldly lusts, we should live soberly (self-controlled), righteously, and godly, in this present world.

[Titus 2:12]

But I keep under my body, and bring it into subjection: lest that by any means, when I have preached to others, I myself should be a castaway.

[1 Corinthians 9:27]

But put ye on the Lord Jesus Christ, and make not provision for the flesh, to fulfil the lusts thereof.

[Romans 13:14]

Divine Name of God

Elohim
(God as Creator)
[Genesis 1:1]

El Shaddai
(More Than Enough)
[Genesis 17:1]

Jehovah-Elyon
(Most High)
[Psalm 7:17]

Jehovah-Jireh
(Provider)
[Genesis 22:4]

Jehovah-Nissi
(Banner)
[Exodus 17:15]

Jehovah-Rapha
(Healer)
[Exodus 15:26]

Jehovah-Rohi
(Shepherd)
[Psalm 23:1]

Jehovah-Shalom
(Peace)
[Judges 6:24]

Jehovah-Shammah
(The Lord Is There)
[Ezekiel 48:35]

Jehovah-Tsidkenu
(Righteous)
[Jeremiah 23:6]

I thank and praise God for wisdom to write my second book.

Now unto him that is able to do exceeding abundantly above all that I ask or think, according to the power that worketh in me.

[Ephesians 3:20]

Thank You Jesus!!!

www.ingramcontent.com/pod-product-compliance
Lightning Source LLC
Chambersburg PA
CBHW021121080526
44587CB00010B/593